GW00725977

Gifts from the Findhorn Gardens

Gifts from the Findhorn Gardens

poems by *Margot Henderson*

photographs by *Adriana Sjan Bijman*

FINDHORN
Press

Poems © Margot Henderson 2005
Photograph of Adriana Sjan Bijman © Kaori Igarashi 2005
All other photographs © Adriana Sjan Bijman 2005
Design by Thierry Bogliolo

First published by Findhorn Press in 2005

Printed and bound in China

Published by
Findhorn Press
305a The Park
Forres IV36 3TE
Scotland, UK
tel 01309-690582/fax 690036
info@findhornpress.com
www.findhornpress.com

Table of Contents

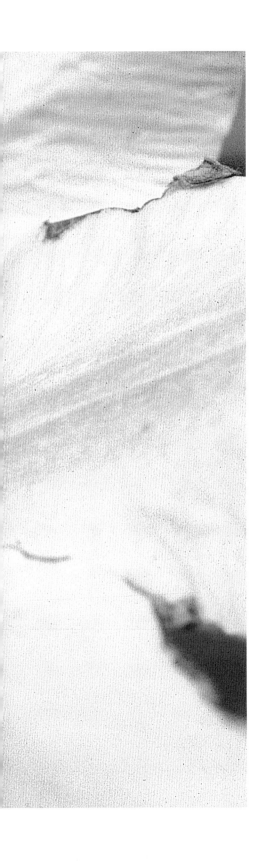

I Open The Book

I open the book of the garden
rain falls with my tears
everything grows here

I am learning
the magic of seeds
and the working cycles of weeds

to be cleared and cleared again
making space
for light spun miracles

I see this is how it is
in me, in all of us,
for we too are cyclical

we too are natural
and our journey into light
is not linear but lyrical

IMBOLC

Ewe's milk   **spring sings**

dawn maiden   **light returning**

sowing seeds   new beginnings

snowdrops rising

Snowdrops Song

Snowdrops are ringing
their little bells

the sound is breaking
winter's spell.

The ice is melting
around my heart

and I feel I'm rising
from the dark.

Onto This Earth

I am falling
onto this earth
gently like rain

I am falling
onto this earth
like grain
scattering

broken like bread
to rise again

I am falling
onto this earth
blown by the wind
each blossom rent

petal by petal
torn from my stem
heart falls trembling

onto this earth

Turnip Seeds

I see at last
the tiny tops
of turnip seeds
opening heart leaves

as baby beetroots beat
their slender purple tips
along their stems

I had almost
given up on them
and then
I realise they are
root vegetables

I forget sometimes
how much growing
is unseen
how much change happens
in the dark

I feel reassured
I don't have to give up
on loving you

there is so much
between us
that I cannot see

so I let go
and grow
into the mystery

Sowing Seeds

Mindfully I sow
these lettuce seeds
and wish them well

wholeness
fullness

the balance
of the elements

the nourishment of soil
soothing rains
gentle air
sunlight in their hearts

As I make these aspirations
I bring to mind
the seeds that I am sowing now

May I sow
seeds of love
and peacefulness
in this moment

in each moment

not the seeds of suffering

Lettuce Seeds

Today I sow the lettuce seeds
in fingerprinted beds
here the baby lettuces
will rest their green and leafy
sleepy heads.

Will they, I wonder,
dream of me

Will they remember me

Will my finger-printed whorls
affect the contours of their curls

Will the touch
of my fingers
influence the lettuces
they come to be.

Putting Baby Beans to Bed

Between the rows of broad beans
I crawl on hands and knees
I am becoming creature
sister to the bugs
that scuttle in the mulch

I am shrinking
smaller than a baby bean stem
I am a child again
my body remembering how to crawl
re-membering myself
as one with the All

I am mother and child
at the same time
as I tuck these baby beans
warm and cosy in their beds
wrapped in blankets of mulch grass
to dream their green bean dreams

Emergence
Creating 'Crane' – the new polytunnel at Cullerne Gardens

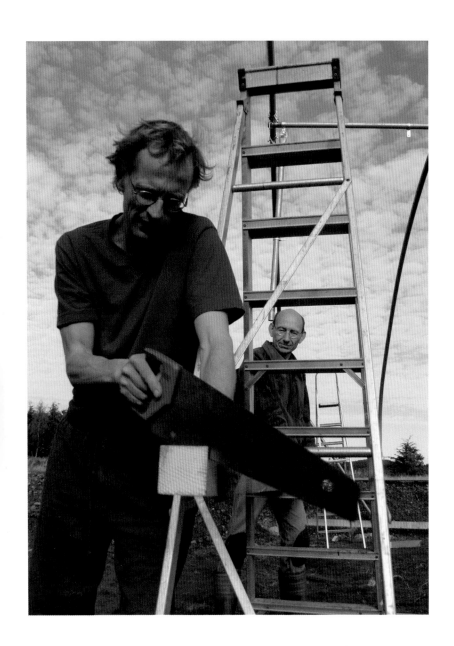

From the jutting jawbone
of a prehistoric creature
rising from the earth
an ancient mouth opens
swallowing the sky
and giving birth

To the hull of a great ship
setting sail across a sea of grass
where a great whale arcs
silver glinting
in each slivered bone
its rib cage cresting
with each rolling wave

A bare boned temple
to the moon and stars
curving across heaven
like the goddess Knut
bowing down to dawn and dusk
and daily giving birth to earth

An embryo
membrane
spinning its own skein of skin
breathing in utero
into the life it will begin

A spaceship
circumnavigating earth
soon to be inhabited
by little green beings
Extraordinary Terrestrials

Cullerne's own Chartres
wall to wall windows
stained with elemental light
Christopher's Cathedral
a testimony
to his devotion and delight.

Morning Call

I step into the garden
into the glory
of the morning
as the oyster catcher calls
'Habib'
a Sufi greeting
to the friend

He dives
into the ocean of me
breaks me open
and retrieves a pearl.

This morning
walking mindfully
in the garden
the sea roars
breathing in and out

Beneath my feet
a grass ocean
rising and falling
like Jesus I walk on water

Sufi Poem
for Kassim

I sat in the tavern
drinking with a Sufi friend

when I came home
I danced barefoot
in the garden

to the music of rain
falling on leaves
and geese calling
across the water

each one tells
their yearning for God
in their own tongue

I step carefully
for the daisies
are star constellations
dervishes dancing in the grass
and the whole world is spinning

Rosebud Nebula Song

There's a rosebud opening
up among the stars.
The universe is blossoming
deep within my heart.

There's a spring coming, so let love in.
There's a spring coming, so get loving.

A hundred baby new born stars
are putting down their roots
in the gardens of the skies
and sending out new shoots.

There's a spring coming, so let love in.
There's a spring coming, so get loving.

Like an arrow from a bow
that flies straight to my heart
the geese are flying overhead
and dancing with the stars.

There's a spring coming, so let love in.
There's a spring coming, so get loving.

Irises (I rises)

Iris swords rise up
to herald spring
how can we
imagine for one moment
that such slender
tender blades of leaves
could pierce their way
unaided through this
dark weight of soil

Left to their own devices
they would be crushed

It is the force of life
the spirit strength within
the fierce light of spring
that rises them

So too when we
feel ourselves to be
immersed in darkness
with the weight of soil
about our heads
it is the light within
it is the I that rises us
I rises

BELTANE

The Green Man   sap rising

flowers blossoming   lengthening of days

summer warming

love lies fertile in the fields

In The Green Hall

In the tunnel
arched like the hall
of a fairy mound,
green within
and green around,
harp strings rise up
from the ground.

Green bean tendrils
twine around my fingers
as I play the strings.
I listen
as the Green Bean Deva sings.

In the Green Lady's chamber
the ladies in waiting spin,
strands of tendril,
strands of string.

Our fingers plait and weave
the tiny threads
a tender tapestry of leaves.

The Humble Bumble Bee

The humble bumble bee
hums its way
into the centre of the rose

straight to the heart of her
bowing
allowing himself to be

enfolded by her petals
he surrenders
totally to her

humming deep inside
his song sounds
from her chamber
resonant

lovers
could learn from him
how to make love
honey

Calendula

I kneel before this calendula and bow
there is a universe inside her
each bud opens
in star formation
with cosmic geometric precision

It is the beginning
of a solar system
each petal uncurling
like starfire
or a comet's tail

The centre is a galaxy
of stars pulsating
I gaze into the maze of her
and I am voyaging
into the infinite
in the infinitesimal

I feel myself become a bee
I be
I being lost
for a moment
in that reverie
I see a bee
has entered her

I wonder for a moment
'Is it me?'
I see him step on stars
the tiny golden stamens of her heart
he dusts his feet
with pollen dancing and we fly

the calendula, the bee and I

Flamenco Poppies

These flamenco poppies
spread their scarlet skirts and twirl.
They flick their leafy fans and spin.

Stamping their stemmed feet
dancing wild steps
to nature's beat.

They toss their dusky gypsy heads
bedecked with jewelled combs.

Their frond fingers
draw admiring suitors close.

They shrug and play them
like so many sets

of castanets.

Iris Geisha Girls

These yellow irises
gather round the garden pond
a group of geishas giggling

pale and slender
green kimonoed
dressed for the summer festival

nodding to each other
chattering among themselves
bowing to the waters
where the lilies rise

Water Lily Dancers

Water Lilies dancing

on the surface of the pond

tutued ballerinas

a chorus of balletic swans

all pirouettes and fluttering

their petal wings

Their arabesques and pas de bas

their pointwork footwork

on slender green stemmed limbs

a secret choreography

beneath the water's surface

out of sight

Each Water Lily rises

like a little mermaid

to the surface

when she comes of age

Opening her petal eyes

she sees the bright Water lily

shining in the ocean of the skies

She opens her lily heart to love

opening her lily throat to sing

the beauty of this world

in each and every

each and every thing

Sweet Peas

Spiral seekers
of the light

Temple dancers
subtle feminine
seducers

Brightly coloured
courtesans

Life weavers
Light weavers

You give yourselves
into our hands

Perfumed priestesses
of the sacred maze

Healer revealers
of stem cell patternings

Dreamer healers
of the nervous system
and the glands

We give ourselves
into your hands

(Sweet) Peas

What could the essence be?
of a simple garden pea.
How from this crescent
green moon oyster shell
a cloistered clustering
a string of bright green pearls.

Carpet Garden

I step between
the rows
of Dahlias
walking on rugs
of carpet mulch

The patterns
reminding me
of childhood
whirling dervish
magic carpets
whooshing me away

I am journeying
through dream mandalas
dhakinis
dragon dancers
in the fireside rugs

The same whirling
in the flower patterns
the same romantic geomantics

The same sacred symmetry
geometry
arising from these
glories of the garden

Cosmos, Aster, Marguerite
Dahlia, Chrysanthemum

as in the wondrous wanderers
in the carpet garden
at my mum's

Darling Dahlia,

Do you know
when you first open
to the warm touch
of sun on your green skin
when first your buds tremble
with the fall of dew

Do you know
when first your flower hearts
burst open
offering your beauty
pouring love and joy
into this world

Do you know
that when the lover chooses you
and takes you in
you will be broken
from the stem
and your life will never be
the same again

Knowing this
do you still choose
to open up your flower heart
to love ?

Dahlia's Reply

I am a flower
not a single bloom or stem
I am the whole flower then
I let myself open to love
over and over again

Each blossom is
a single love
that has its time to live

Each has its own expression
its unique gift to give
When the bloom has faded
there is no cause
for shame or blame

I simply draw my life force
back into my stem
draw it deep down
into my roots
till it is time to bloom again

For the force of love is greater
than a single flower
the source of love is greater
than any other power

It simply is our nature
to give and receive love
to grow from earth
and rise to heaven above

The Family Garden

On Sunday I visit the Family Garden
choosing to spend time with real relations
choosing to converse with relatives.
Cousin carrots, sister spinaches
who are quiet and chattering by turns.

I pay my familial respects
to great grandmothers and grandfathers
who may once have been
and now may seem
poppies or irises, turnips or radishes.

I listen respectfully
when they tell me,
" We all have our roots in this same earth.
We all have our feet in this same soil
and we would do well to remember it."

Potato aunts and uncles
reach out their green leafed hands
to greet me open palmed
veined like my own skin
flesh of my own flesh
as I take them in.

They tell me stories of the old days
whispering of journeys
from strange continents
and far flung places.
Shaking their flowery heads
as they remember
lean times on a green isle
famine and scarcity.

The little daisy nieces
are in their flowerbed rooms
dressing up in frilly petticoats
playing hide and seek ,
peek-a-boo and kiss chases.

They are all my family
with their 10,000 faces.

Lovely Lady Anthemis

Lovely Lady Anthemis
shines golden as the sun
she tidies all her petals up
when her shining time is done

She is an origami artist
with her petals in neat folds
tucked away like little wings
beneath her crown of gold

Star Gazer Lilies

They gather
like a flock of swans
slender stalked
long necked
wing fanned
and fluttering

They are positively biblical
full of faith in themselves
all angel swords
shrill trumpeting
and glory hallelujahing
from their heavenly
choiring throats

They are perfect lovers
well versed in tantric arts
perfectly harmonious
in their display
of male and female parts

They are perfumed courtesans
promising and fulfilling
sensual bliss

They are divine mazes
star gazers
proclaiming joyously
what is

Good News

Friday 27th June 2003
the world turns inside
my heart skips a beat
for there on the front page
of the quality news
is a photograph
of a healthy heart
and I can't help hoping
this might be the start
of good news for a change

Just how good can good news be
its not even relegated to page 3
the full frontal
naked unashamed beauty
of our internal human anatomy

I am reading The Guardian
straight from the garden
so when I look at this image
I can't help but see
a plant tuber with a tangle of roots
a seed pod bursting with shoots

This picture seems to me
to be the living proof
of what I have always believed
this earth is the womb
in which we were truly conceived

When I see this good news
I can't help being affected
by the imprint, the in-print
of how all things are connected
our plant selves our planet selves
how our hearts are planted
in our bodies' soil
how they flower in our actions
in this world

LAMMAS

Earth's goldening   harvest ripening
gathering in   the sacred marriage

flower and fruit   **deep fulfillment**

the time of turning leaves

The Angel of Cullerne Song

As the Autumn days turn golden
and the leaves come falling down
we give thanks for the holding
as the year is turning round

We give thanks for the harvest
all the fruits of this garden
and we give thanks to the Angel
The Angel of Cullerne

Each one of these
is an enchanted forest
full of magic
pop-up trees

Each one of these
is an atlas
each leaf page
maps the journeys
the ordinance of the underground
pathways rootways
and tributaries

Each one of these
is a body
with its own veins
and arteries
each leaf a heart
pulsing with capillaries

Each one of these
is a life
when I cut you
there are traces
of my blood on your knife

Each one of these
is a stained glass window
equal to those
in the Cathedral at Chartres
each one crafted
by the ultimate artist

Red Chard

To A Courgette

From that first thrusting from the seed
it was clear you had an urgent need to be
free of all constraints.
You pushed your roots through the seedcase
like some shellfish creature, blindly reaching
for the sea.

Then you lay
between the sheets
of moist newspapers
between the black and white
as you stretched out your stems
in search of light.

I looked at you and then I knew
that you were fierce green angels
dancing with delight into this life.
You unravelled as you revelled
in the joy of simply being you.

Now in the fields
you put yourselves about
your yellow joyous trumpets sounding out
the music for your circle dance.
A perfect choreography of male and female parts
combining potent and seductive arts.
Trumpets rising in crescendo
as you reach the peak of sexual inuendo

Like a mother I watch your earthly dance with pride.
The sheen upon your skin
reflects the shining light inside.
Leaf arms stretch warm and wide to reach us.
Heart opening to teach us,

'Rejoice. The life force cannot be denied.'

Tomato Teachings in The Tao...

If it is hard
don't try to force.
It means it isn't ripe yet.

Intensity of colour
is a good sign of readiness
and willingness to yield.

If it does not come to you easily
it may not be yours for the picking.
Some things are worth waiting for

Pay attention.
Simplicity of form
can be deceptive.

It may be an outward sign
of an essential nature
full of wholeness
and great depth.

Do not be fooled by appearances.
See how the flower
gives way for the fruit.

At a certain point
it becomes necessary
to curtail branching out
on new ventures.

It is vital to conserve energy
to nourish the ripening fruit.

Remember every outer form
no matter how ordinary
conceals and yet reveals
the mystery.
The All that lies within
the secret seeds
of the 10,000 things.

Cucumber Devas

Let us teach you of being
that which is beyond your seeing
As you look on these cucumber stems
you see a life cycle coming to an end
you see withered, torn leaves
spotted and crumpled with disease
but we are not these.
Our power is the energy you feel
rising from the ground.
Our power is the energy you are sensing
all around.
Our's the power that confounds
those who believe
that spirit leaves.
Do not be fooled by the decay and death
that is before your eyes
feel into the truth
that spirit never dies.
If anything, the life force in us
is stronger now
as we gather it back into ourselves
now that we are not engaged
in dividing and creating visible cells
This peace is the peace you find
in cemeteries
this peace is the peace
of autumn trees
the deep peace
of soul's release
rest as we now rest
in peace.

Picking Broad Beans

Breathing in bean
breathing out bean

Bean being
broad bean

not bored bean
or brood bean

but broad bean
bean wholly being

Breathing in being
breathing out being

Human being
broad being

not bored being
or brood being
but wholly being

Not might have been
or having been
being wholly being

Bean being
human being
both being

Interbeing
wholly being
holy being

Original Garden

Mindful walking
in the original garden
I meet the plants again

I am rapt
in Lady's Mantle
held within her folds
of green leaf sky
and raindrop constellation

I am woven
in the web
of a nasturtian leaf
held from falling
by a tracery of veins
spun from the centre
of her heart to mine

Meanwhile poppy stems
have shed their scarlet
and their purple cloaks
for it is time

to show themselves
as wise and comical
crone queens

I bow to them
stripped bare of every thing
but this and now

When you step up intae
That rickety green caravan
Or find that cardboard box
Left by your door
Remember that it's no
Just fruit and vegetables
You hold in your two hands
O no, it's so much more.

It's no just cabbages, tatties,
spinach, neeps and broad beans.
It's no just tomatoes, courgettes
and cucumbers, it's also what it means
It's no just vegetables they're growing here
It's dreams.

It's sunlight, soil and wind and rain
It's life risin up through earth, in us,
Over an over an over again.
And it's wet feet, cold hands,
Sweatin labour an the odd back pain.

It's not just a couple o fields and a garden
Somewhere in the heart o Morayshire.
It's nothin short o being miraculous
They're feedin us.
By their desire to choose the good
They grow the food that we require.
It's a statement, a commitment
To both nourish and inspire.

EarthShare*
Celebration
Poem

It is a gift.
Not just to the locals who subscribe
Not just to the Moray EarthShare tribe
But to everybody everywhere.
It's livin proof that we can make trade fair.
It's livin proof
That it doesn't cost a lot to care.
It's the livin truth
That the Earth is ours to share.

So when you tuck intae
Your EarthShare box
Spare a thought for the farmers
In their mucky wellies and their soggy socks
And let's all put our money where our mouth is
Let's all stand up and walk our talk

And when your delicious organic dinner's
Steamin and gleamin on your plate
Take a wee minute just to celebrate
These farmers
And this earth that we all share.
These farmers and this Earth that we all share.

*EarthShare is the local organic
community support agriculture
scheme feeding up to 200 families
every week. It has been in operation
for eleven years now making it the
oldest one in Scotland.

Basil Song

You teach us
How precious life is
How tender
And how sweet

You are trusting
Like little children
Opening your hearts
Opening your arms

Berry Picking Song

As the season draws to an end
we pick the berries from the stem
Before the bush we bow our heads
as we pick the jewels of black and red
We sing as those who went before
for each we pick may there be more
for each we pick may there be more

Seed Pods

Chinese lanterns

Russian Orthodox Church domes

Golden Mosque cuppolas

tiny gold and silver boats
sailing seeds downstream

little faerie baskets
full of seeds
to take to harvest market

Calendula caterpillars
curling up to sleep

Quietly At Dusk

I tiptoe through the garden
quietly at dusk
so as not to wake
the flowers in their beds

I slip softly past
the compost rows
tucked and snuggled in
beneath their blankets
for the night

I pause a moment
and I seem to feel them breathe
a dormitory full of sleeping giants
with tufty grass and curly cabbage heads
resting on the pillow
of the rich brown earth

I watch them and wonder
do they dream me walking by ?
Or in their loamy turning
do they only dream
of the plants and flowers
that will one day

rise through them ?

Little Chard Angel Song

A little chard angel
with folded wings
no longer watches
over the fields
the harvest is over now
and her job is done
so she can fly away
back to the One

SAMHAIN

The Hag, Old Crone
who wraps us in Her deep cloak of winter

darkening the drawing in
wild weather dreaming rest

Into the Silence

Birds sing
into the silence
as the sea
sighs everything

wild geese
fly overhead
all trumpeting
and beating wings
to settle on the river

Fading poppies
spread their tattered skirts
and dance
and dance
into the darkness

As I step
barefoot
on the path
wherever
it will lead me

Reflection

Looking in the pond
I see myself
in everything
and everything in me.

I am the sky
sun, cloud, tree.

This world wears my face.
I am this place.

Looking in the pond
my hair trails in the water
indistinguishable from fronds.

Lilies rise up in me.
Breeze fingers ripple me.

I am in utter bliss.
I am inseparable from this .

Gardeners in All Weathers

We come and go
like clouds
drifting
inside
outside
across the sky
across the earth
according to the weather

Gorse on The Dunes

Huddled together on the dune's edge
they bow their backs
against the winds
twisted by the buffetting
skin cracked by salt and weathering.

Gnarled branched crone fingers
point in all directions
warding off.
They scry the sky and prophesy.

Faded grey green guardians
they are still
fierce keepers of their golden flames

Green in Snow

Like a simple scholar
I peruse each page
of ornamental greens
written in the soil trays

Each one a poem composed
of precise pictograms
each character perfectly
defined
takes its place within
the ideogrammic lines

These plants are haiku
small and compact
yet they contain
enough green leafage
to maintain
a whole community
throughout the winter

Each one its own word
silently yet perfectly
uttering the essence of itself
Tat Soy , Pak Choi
Komatsuna , Mizuna
Namenia , Quarantina
Words written
through the winter
green in snow

The Bell Sounding

In the garden, waiting
I listen for the bell.

Birdsong. The bell sounds.
Wind in the trees. The bell sounds.
Rain falls. The bell sounds.

A hammer tapping gently
the gardener's footsteps on the grass
voices in the distance.

What is this waiting ?

The whole world is a bell sounding
inviting wakefulness.

Smiling in the centre of myself
I am the bell sounding

Listen. In the centre of your self
you are a bell sounding.

Pine Trees Tai Chi

Stand strong
you have your roots in the earth
as we do.
All things have their source
in the invisible.
Embody power
in the trunk
Rise up.
Reach out.
Send your spirit forth
into this world.
See what can grow
from your fingertips.
Trust your own unfolding
as we do.
Bow down
see these wild flowers
growing out of bare rock.
Such is this earth
All things are possible.
Embrace earth.
Embrace heaven.
Believe.
Be leaf.
All life
Is utterly miraculous.

Heather

We are many manifold spinners and weavers.
From this soil we draw the threads
the warp and weft of colour, light, pattern and form.
We clothe this land, drawing down the light
the subtlety of shade and shadow.
We hold and herald seasons' turn
the fall of light, the movement of the sun.

We are hale and hearty.
We bring healing, luck and cheerfulness.
We are wanderers like the travellers
who tie us up in bunches
and sell us for good fortune.

We are the softening, the brightening
of wild habitation.
A comfort to the human
in the face of what may seem
like barren desolation.
We know how to live through changing form
and myriad incarnations.
We take many subtle forms in splendid variations.

We rejoice in bloom and in the quiet times
of emptying and goldening.
Letting go of seeds, dying to the outer form
that new life can be born.

I Dance For The Plants

I dance for the plants
for their sacred geometric forms
their heart shaped petals
their star-form patterns
their spirals, their cycles and their
cells.

I dance for the plants
in the Universal Hall
and I see that we are all
seeds scattering
infused with sacred patterning
within this holy place
We are flowers emerging
from this cosmic seed case

I dance for the plants
wild gypsy dances
dervishing and spiralling
my steps are Celtic, Middle Eastern
Indian and African
for they are all the same
invoking life upon this earth
invoking the growth of plants
with every step

I dance for the plants
and see I do not dance alone
we are all plants dancing
and this garden is our home

The Angel of Scotland

I am the bringer of rainbows
dancer in the doorway
between earth, sky and sea

I am keeper of the wilderness
defender of fierce beauty

I am the tender
of tiny heather bells
and thistledown
into whose cups I pour
the colours of the dawn

I dance at the edge of time
ancient, awesome
in me you know
the truth of being alone
of walking, spirit, free

I am maker of fine distinctions
between strengthened force
depth and heaviness
grief and longing

I am utter purity
aloneness and all-one-ness
light and density

Gardener God

I have been shaken
from my stem

a seed blown in the wind
into another garden

Help me to grow strong
and flourish

Help me to flower
in full fragrance

May I be a joy
to all who come by me

May I open to the sun
being all that I am

May gentle humming bees
sing songs in me

gather my pollen
and make honey of me

And in the season of fading
may I rest in the earth

May I rest in the earth
to rise again

Margot Henderson is a poet, storyteller and community artist who has generated arts and education projects for the last 25 years supporting diverse groups and organisations in their creative processes. Much of her work has been site specific celebrating nature and our connection with it. Since returning to Scotland in 2002 she has continued this work alongside working as a volunteer in Cullerne Gardens and contributing to Findhorn Foundation Programmes and Community Celebrations.

With particular thanks and blessings to

Dorothy MacLean for *Falling in Love with God* and for opening
the hearts of all she meets to the Divinity in Nature.

Eileen and Peter Caddy for holding true to
the vision and grounding it on earth

The Bards who have given voice to the beauty of the land

All the Gardeners, particularly the Cullerne garden team
for all their loving work on this good earth

Karin, Thierry and all at Findhorn Press for helping
us to realize the dream of the book

Sabine for helping to make it so

For three decades **Adriana Sjan Bijman** has been working as a photographer/artist/designer. Born in Holland, she has studied art in Amsterdam and has worked in organic farming, the women's movement, the environment movement and in nature. She resonates with the old European and matriarchal traditions as present in the Celtic rituals and stories. Through her images as well as in her range of photo-cards she tries to communicate the Beauty of Nature, the Divine Gift of our planet. Since 1998 she has been living and working in the Findhorn Foundation. See more of her work on www.findhorn.org/adriana.html

The Findhorn Garden

by *The Findhorn Community*

A brand new edition with new chapter bringing the story up to date!

Over 40 years ago, on windswept and barren sand dunes in the far north east of Scotland, a miracle was occurring. The most wonderful plants, flowers, trees and organic vegetables were growing to enormous sizes in a small plot around a thirty-foot caravan trailer inhabited by three adults and three children living on £8 a week unemployment benefit. Guidance by God and absolute faith in the art of manifestation led them to this apparently unlikely place to create a magnetic centre which, they were told, would draw people from all over the world. Their discovery of how to contact and cooperate with nature spirits and devas made the seemingly impossible possible. The Findhorn phenomenon had begun.

Today, that same caravan stands in tribute to the pioneering faith of its former residents, amid a thriving village housing hundreds of people from all over the world; alongside an organisation recognised internationally as a leading centre for spiritual learning, and surrounded by innovative and ecological businesses. The garden has expanded and spawned a huge organic farming initiative feeding hundreds of people. And all this because of the commitment and dedication of those three founders, Eileen and Peter Caddy and Dorothy Maclean.

The Findhorn Community is a living demonstration of what can come about when man co-operates with nature and the beings of higher worlds; when people are united by a common goal based on social, spiritual and ecological values. This is co-creation at its finest. The Findhorn garden is where it all started and this book explores the relationships with angelic realms and devas which first gained the community international recognition, while also looking at the wider work of the community and its huge impact upon all who visit.

available from your local bookshop, or directly from
www.findhornpress.com

ISBN 1-84409-018-3 — 208 pages paperback — many black & white photographs